VETERANS DAY

by Robin Nelson

first step nonfiction

Lerner Publications Company · Minneapolis

We **celebrate** Veterans Day
every year.

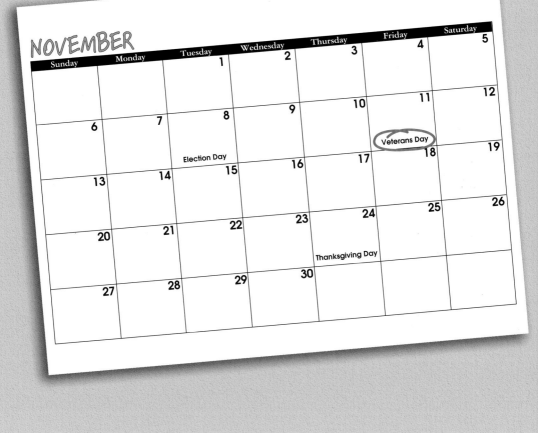

This holiday is in November.

A **veteran** is a person who has served in the **military.**

On Veterans Day, we **honor** people who have fought for our country.

Veterans Day began many
years ago.

America was fighting in
World War I.

On November 11, 1918,
World War I ended.

People celebrated.

This day became Armistice
Day.

Armistice means to stop
fighting.

10	11
	Veterans Day
17	18

Many years later, the holiday was changed to Veterans Day.

Veterans Day honors
veterans from all wars.

We celebrate Veterans Day
at **ceremonies.**

We go to parades.

People wear flowers.

We thank and honor all veterans.

Veterans Day Timeline

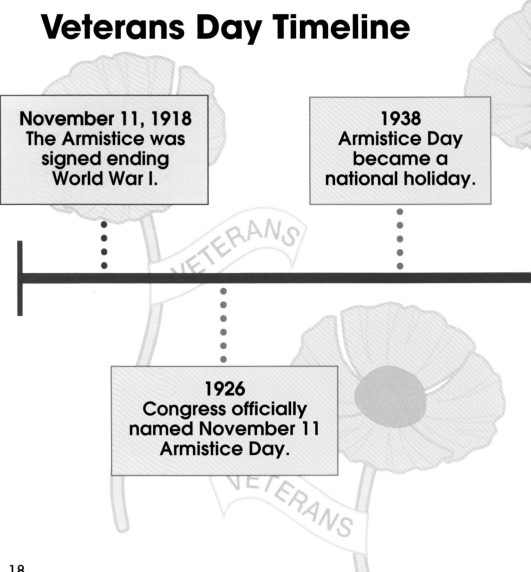

November 11, 1918
The Armistice was
signed ending
World War I.

1938
Armistice Day
became a
national holiday.

1926
Congress officially
named November 11
Armistice Day.

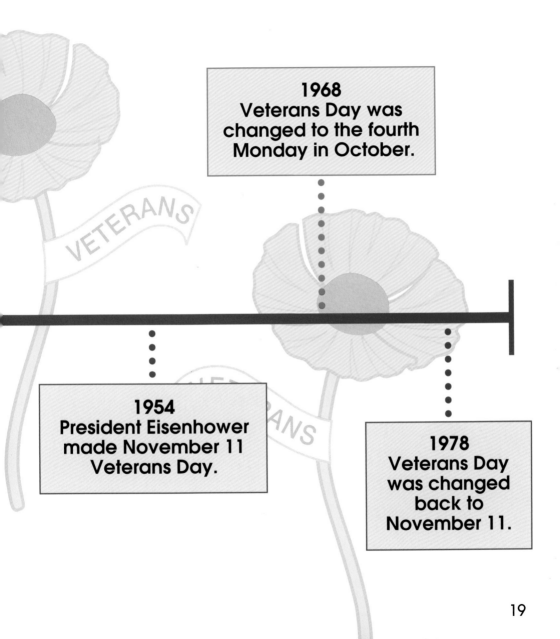

1968
Veterans Day was changed to the fourth Monday in October.

1954
President Eisenhower made November 11 Veterans Day.

1978
Veterans Day was changed back to November 11.

Veterans Day Facts

 Veterans Day is celebrated every year on November 11.

 Some people wear a special flower on Veterans Day. They wear a poppy to remember those who have died in battle.

 In 1968, Veterans Day was changed to the fourth Monday in October. Americans wanted to keep the holiday on November 11. It was changed back in 1978.

In Great Britain and France, Veterans Day is still called Armistice Day. In Canada, it is called Remembrance Day.

There is a special ceremony at the Tomb of the Unknown Soldier every Veterans Day. The tomb is in Washington, D.C. The president of the United States talks and puts a wreath on the tomb.

Glossary

 celebrate – to have a party or special activity to honor a special occasion

ceremonies – formal acts to honor an event or special occasion

 honor – to show special respect for

 military – a nation's armed forces

 veteran – a person who has served in the armed forces